The story of potjiekos

MADE IN SOUTH AFRICA

Lynn Barnes

Words that are in bold, like **this**, are explained in the Word help, on the page and at the end of the book.

The *Made in South Africa* series is published by
Awareness Publishing Group (Pty) Ltd.
Copyright © 2019

Awareness Publishing (SA) (Pty) Ltd
www.awareness.co.za
info@awareness.co.za
+27 (0)86 110 1491
www.facebook.com/AwarenessPublishing

All rights reserved. No part of this publication may be reproduced in any form without written permission from the publisher, except by a reviewer.

First edition 2019

The story of potjiekos by Lynn Barnes
ISBN 978-1-77008-993-8

Summary: A simple introduction to potjiekos, including what it is, a little about its history, and how to make it.

Book design: Richard Keenan-Smith and Elizabeth Barnard

Editorial credits: Managing editor: Monique le Riché; Copy editor: Danya Ristić-Schacherl; Picture editors: Anne Laing and Lawrence Frank

Picture credits: Cover © Jeremy Glyn; cover (background) © Jeremy Glyn; cover (flag) © Kurt / Dreamstime; endpapers © Jeremy Glyn; p4 © AAI FotoStock SA / Alamy / Agencja Fotograficzna Caro; p6 © Gallo Images / Getty Images / Popperfoto; p8 (top) © Gallo Images / Getty Images / Universal History Archive; p8 (bottom) © Iziko Museum / Independent Contributors / Africa Media Online; p10 (top) © Gallo Images / Getty Images / Universal History Archive; p10 (bottom) © Gallo Images / Getty Images / Universal History Archive; p12 © AAI FotoStock SA / Jeff Greenberg; p14 © Imagesbybarbara / iStock; p16 © ruvanboshoff / iStock; p18 © Lynn Barnes; p20 © Jeremy Glyn; p22 © Henti Smith; p24 © Jan van der Poll; p26 © Jeremy Glyn; p28 © Anne Laing; p28 (inset) © SMART GECKO SOFTWARE DEVELOPMENT; p30 © Jeremy Glyn; p32 © Jeremy Glyn; p34 © Jeremy Glyn; p36 © Jeremy Glyn; p38 © Paul Weinberg / South Photos / Africa Media Online

1 3 5 7 9 0 8 6 4 2

Contents

Eating outdoors 5
Cooking in iron pots 7
Cooking on the move 9
Hunting 11
Unique to SA 13
Differences between potjiekos and stew – 1 15
Differences between potjiekos and stew – 2 17
The pot 19
Make your own potjiekos 21
The fire 23
Other ways to heat the pot 25
Ingredients 27
Recipes 29
"Building a potjie" 31
Listen to the potjie "talk" 33
Checking the pot 35
Share with friends 37
Word help 39

South Africa has good weather for cooking outdoors.

Eating outdoors

South Africa has good weather and many people like to spend time outdoors. They also enjoy cooking outdoors. One way of doing this is to make potjiekos. "Potjiekos" (we say: POY-kee-koss) is an Afrikaans word made up of two parts: *potjie* means "little pot" and *kos* means "food". So *potjiekos* is "little pot food" or "food made in a little pot".

Four Zulu men eating a meal made in an iron pot in 1910.

Cooking in iron pots

People in South Africa have been cooking in iron pots for hundreds of years. The first settlers who came from the Netherlands, in Europe, in the 1800s brought their heavy, black iron pots with them. They cooked their food in the pots hanging from hooks over a fire.

Even before these settlers arrived, the African farmers who were moving into southern Africa had learnt to use iron pots from traders who visited Africa.

A drawing from 1895 showing an ox-wagon with a potjie hanging underneath.

A drawing done in 1839 showing Voortrekkers cooking in a potjie.

Cooking on the move

Potjiekos began with the Voortrekkers who travelled across the country in ox-wagons in the 1800s and 1900s. They kept their cooked food inside the pots and fastened them under their wagons while they were travelling. When they stopped for the night, they put the pots back on the fire and warmed up the food again.

A hunter hunting buck in a picture from the 1800s.

Some parts of the buck hanging from the trees would end up in the pot underneath.

Hunting

The Voortrekkers made a kind of **stew** with meat, including the large bones, and whatever vegetables they could find. The bones added flavour and made the stew thicker.

> **Word help**
> **stew:** a kind of thick soup made of meat and vegetables cooked slowly in liquid in a pot with a lid

The Voortrekkers had to hunt for their food on their journey. The men hunted small game such as buck, guinea fowl, bush pigs and rabbits. They added the fresh meat to the pot and changed the older bones for new bones.

A group of people enjoying potjiekos.

Unique to SA

Nowadays, potjiekos is a South African speciality. It is usually cooked over an open fire outside, often with a group of friends.

It is not necessary to use expensive meat. In fact, cheaper, fattier meat works better because the slow cooking makes it very tasty and **tender**.

> **Word help**
> **tender:** soft and easy to eat, not tough and chewy

Once the food is in the pot, it needs no attention. So everyone can sit around the fire, chatting and relaxing and enjoying the wonderful smells of the food cooking.

Stew has a lot of liquid.

Differences between potjiekos and stew - 1

Both stew and potjiekos contain meat and vegetables and are cooked in a pot with a lid. But there are two main differences.

A stew has a lot of liquid and it does not matter if the lid is lifted during cooking.

But not much liquid is added to potjiekos, and the lid is kept closed during cooking. So the food cooks in the steam inside the pot rather than boiling in the liquid as a stew does.

Potjiekos does not have much liquid.

Differences between potjiekos and stew – 2

A stew is stirred so that the **ingredients** are mixed together and the whole stew has the same flavour.

> **Word help**
> **ingredients:** the things used to make something, especially when cooking

The ingredients in potjiekos are added in layers and are not stirred during the cooking. So they do not mix together and the flavours are kept separate.

There are many different sizes of potjies.

The pot

The pots, or "potjies", used for making potjiekos are made from a heavy metal called iron. They are usually black and round, and have three little legs. These pots are available in many shops, and come in many sizes, from tiny to huge.

The most popular sizes are numbers 2, 3 and 4.

Ask an adult to help you make your potjiekos.

Make your own potjiekos

If you would like to try to make your own potjiekos, it is very important that you find an adult to help you. Making a fire and cooking over it can be very dangerous. <u>Do not try to do this on your own.</u>

A potjie full of food can also be very heavy, so you may need an adult to help you carry it.

The pot should sit on the hot coals, not directly on the flames.

The fire

The fire is an important part of making potjiekos. It does not matter whether you use wood or charcoal, as long as you can control the heat of the fire. This is done by moving more **coals** under the pot to increase the heat. Or by moving some coals away from the pot to reduce the heat.

> **Word help**
>
> **coals:** the hot, burning part of a fire without any flames

The coals need to be ready before you start cooking, so allow time for the fire to burn first. It is a good idea to divide your fire into two parts so that you have extra coals to put under the pot if needed.

> **Important**
>
> Remember to get an adult to help you.

You can put the pot on a gas burner or on a special holder over a gas bottle.

Other ways to heat the pot

Traditionally, the potjie is heated over an open fire built on the ground. But you can build the fire anywhere that is safe. You could even build a special place in your garden for cooking. Just make sure that the fire cannot spread and cause damage.

> **Word help**
>
> **traditionally:** in the way that something is usually done and has been done for a long time

You can also heat your potjie using gas. You can put the potjie on a stand over a gas ring or use one of the special holders that fit onto a gas bottle.

Make sure you have everything ready before you start making your potjiekos.

Ingredients

The main ingredients are usually:

- meat – for example beef, lamb, pork or chicken
- vegetables – for example onions, carrots, butternut, baby marrows, mushrooms, potatoes, peeled (if needed) and chopped into pieces

You will also need:

- cooking oil
- seasonings – for example garlic, salt, pepper, herbs and spices
- 1 or 2 cups of liquid, such as water or fruit juice. Some people believe that using Coca-Cola, beer or wine makes the potjiekos taste even better.

Some people like to put in fruit, such as chopped apple or canned sliced peaches.

You can put in whatever you like or have available.

You can find potjiekos recipes in cookery books.
Inset: There is even a potjiekos recipe app that you can download to a cellphone or tablet.

Recipes

There are many recipes for making potjiekos. Cooks often have their own special recipes and secrets for making it. You can find recipes in cookery books or on the **Internet**.

> **Word help**
> **Internet:** a system that links computers all over the world and where you can find information on many things

You could look in your local library for books with potjiekos recipes, or ask family members and friends for ideas.

Or you can experiment by making up your own recipe.

Add your ingredients in layers to "build your potjie".

"Building a potjie"

Because the ingredients are put into the pot in layers, people call it "building a potjie".

- Put some oil into the potjie. Put the potjie on the fire to get hot.
- Add the meat and turn it in the hot oil until it is brown all over. This keeps in the flavour.
- Add the onions and flavourings, stir and cook for a few minutes.
- Add the liquid.
- Then add the vegetables in layers. Start with the harder vegetables, such as carrots and butternut, which take longer to cook. End with the softer ones, such as mushrooms and baby marrows, that cook more quickly.

You can tell by the way your potjie "talks" if it is cooking properly.

Listen to the potjie "talk"

Once you have put all the ingredients in the pot, do not stir them. Just put on the lid and let the food cook slowly. The heavy lid is important because it keeps the steam inside the pot to cook the food.

Check every now and again to make sure it is cooking gently. If the pot is bubbling and hissing, the fire is too hot. You should hear just a gentle bubbling, with a bubble every few seconds. So listen to your potjie "talk" and make changes to the fire when necessary.

If the potjiekos is looking too dry, you can add some water.

Checking the pot

The potjiekos will take several hours to cook if the fire is right. Do not keep taking off the lid and looking in the pot.

You can lift the lid every hour or so to make sure that there is still enough liquid in the pot. If it looks too dry, add some water. But pour the water into the pot down the side, not in the middle.

Be patient!

Enjoy your delicious potjiekos with your friends!

Share with friends

The best way to enjoy potjiekos is with a group of friends. Each person can bring something to put in the pot.

You will need a pot. If you do not have one, perhaps you can borrow one.

First get your fire ready. Next "build your potjie" and put on the lid. Then you can sit back and relax or play some games while the food cooks slowly over the fire.

When the potjiekos is ready, take off the lid, stir the food to mix it, and serve it up.

Enjoy!

Word help

coals: the hot, burning part of a fire without any flames

ingredients: the things used to make something, especially when cooking

Internet: a system that links computers all over the world and where you can find information on many things

stew: a kind of thick soup made of meat and vegetables cooked slowly in liquid in a pot with a lid

tender: soft and easy to eat, not tough and chewy

traditionally: in the way that something is usually done and has been done for a long time